AF421812

Melody's Masterpiece

Miekhail E. Shiver

Copyright © 2024 by
Miekhail E shiver

ALL RIGHTS RESERVED. No part of this book may be reproduced or transmitted in any form by any means, electronic or mechanical, including photocopying and recording, or by any information storage and retrieval system, except as may be expressly permitted in writing from the author.

Printed in the United States of America
Published by Bookmarketeers.com

Planet Scales was a happy place
to be.
On it, there was music
Everywhere to see!

The birds, the dogs, the cats,
the ducklings,

All could whistle, tap dance,
strum and sing!

But Melody the turtle didn't know what to do;

Her name means song, yet she couldn't even cock-a-doodle-doo!

Her friend the cat suggested she "Mew".

But that just gave her throat a boo-boo.

meowR!
me-ouch

Then one day, the chickens all
cooing, said,
"Why don't you try your hand
at composing?"

So Melody used a pencil and her wit...

click click
click click

To write the most beautiful song,
No doubt about it!

I dedicate this book to my friends Andrew and Victoria for inspiring me to go for my dream of writing a book. Thank you!

www.ingramcontent.com/pod-product-compliance
Lightning Source LLC
Chambersburg PA
CBHW042137110726
48006CB00003B/909

9798330232437